T0002503

DEAR Washington, how I love you,
with your beautiful, broad,
generous streets and blue skies!
The sun shines always there for me.

—*from* Personal Memoirs
of Julia Dent Grant, *1975*

ure some ~~Stock~~ Stockings for the
been almost angry with william
uppled with Cloaths, do you think he
t went to commencement in those
e sure, were proper enough for com
had others & with him, to go into so
d so dust. it mortified me — but ct
derations — I send my little evoice a
d it untill I bought it, there is no
usefull hifeans. but some which I d
pprove of — I will never consent
sidered in an inferiour point of lig
shine in their own orbit, god an
if man is Lord, woman is Lordess
& contend for, and if a woman does
government, I see no reason of t f
as they are conducted —
                              when you r
ll easily know the part alluded to
                                 I am my d
ove and affection ever yours
                              A Adam
v a kind
and to John whose turn to commen
as —

SMITHSONIAN
Book of
FIRST LADIES' QUOTATIONS

SMITHSONIAN BOOKS · WASHINGTON, DC

Published by Smithsonian Books
Director: Carolyn Gleason
Senior Editor: Jaime Schwender
Editor: Julie Huggins

Designed by Robert L. Wiser

This book may be purchased for educational, business, or sales promotional use. For information, please write:

Special Markets Department, Smithsonian Books, PO Box 37012, MRC 513, Washington, DC 20013

Library of Congress Cataloging-in-Publication Data available.

ISBN: 978-1-58834-773-2

Printed in the United States of America

28   27   26   25   24   1   2   3   4   5

Library of Congress: page 2, Abigail Adams letter to her sister Elizabeth Smith Shaw Peabody, July 19, 1799. National Museum of American History, Division of Political History: page 6, Eleanor Roosevelt radio address; 19, Louisa Adams platter, photo by Richard Strauss; 27, Mary Todd Lincoln timepiece, photo by Hugh Talman; 30, Frances Cleveland advertisement; 49, Pat Nixon button; and 60, Michelle Obama garden shears, photo by Jaclyn Nash. National Museum of American History & Smithsonian Institution Archives: page 9, Helen "Nellie" Taft inaugural gown, photo by Hugh Talman. National Portrait Gallery: cover, Eleanor Parke Custis silhouette of Martha Washington, ca. 1798; and page 12, Martha Washington portrait after Gilbert Stuart. For permission to reproduce illustrations appearing in this book, please correspond directly with the owners of the works.

Contents

Eleanor Roosevelt addresses the people of the United States
in New York City on August 19, 1945.

Introduction

IT CAN be difficult to find the voices of the first ladies of the United States. Unlike presidents, they do not begin their time in office by giving a public speech. For most of the years that the position has existed, it was considered unseemly for the first lady to express any opinions in public and certainly to comment on public matters. In her biography of her mother, Margaret Truman relates the story of Bess, while Harry was a US senator, telling his cousin Ethel Noland that, for political wives, "a woman's place in public is to sit beside her husband, be silent, and be sure her hat is on straight." Although their voices may have been lowered or sometimes muffled, first ladies have seldom been silent. Their words are found in letters and diaries written before, during, and after their time in the White House as well as in memoirs and reminiscences of friends and family. More recently we hear them in public speeches, interviews, and social media. As you will see in this collection, first ladies have voiced their thoughts on current events, given advice, vented frustrations, and celebrated, deliberated, consoled, and inspired friends, family, and the American people.

The words of first ladies before the twentieth century are hardest to find. Although there were exceptions to the rule—authors, speakers, and activists— most women did not have access to public forums. Public opinion was that women should, as the old saying held, have their names appear in public only three times: when they were born, married, and died. Women who expressed their opinions in public ran the risk of criticism not just for their words but for being unladylike and bad role models for young girls. This was especially true for first ladies, who were expected to be the most refined and reticent examples of American womanhood.

Beginning with Martha Washington, first ladies have been uncomfortable under public scrutiny and high but often undefined public expectations. On her way to join the new president in New York, Lady Washington, as she was called, gave public thanks to the troops accompanying her on the journey and for the warm greetings that she received along the way.[1] Her remarks were reported positively in newspapers, but the same papers and public later made Martha Washington sometimes feel, as she wrote in a letter to her niece Fanny Bassett Washington, "more like a state prisoner than anything else." Perhaps it was that fear of scrutiny and judgment that spurred her to burn almost all her correspondence with her husband after his death, protecting the words of both from public scrutiny. More than 150 years later, Bess Truman, who guarded her privacy as first lady, also burned some of her letters to her husband. When Harry objected, asking her to "think of history," the former first lady responded, "I am."[2]

In the twentieth century, first ladies began to speak publicly. They used speaking engagements and media to lend their support to causes near to their hearts and make connections with the American people. Helen Taft publicly supported woman suffrage and greater

Helen "Nellie" Taft donated this gown, which she wore to her
husband's 1909 inauguration, to the Smithsonian in 1912.
She was the first sitting first lady to donate her inaugural gown,
starting a tradition that every first lady since has followed.

career opportunities for women.[3] Lou Hoover was the first to use radio to connect with listeners, broadcasting talks to boys and girls clubs to promote physical fitness and shared responsibilities between boys and girls.[4] Eleanor Roosevelt expanded the use of radio and used the airwaves along with press conferences, speeches, and her newspaper columns to reach out to the public throughout the Great Depression and World War II with messages of hope, advice, and calls to action.

Modern first ladies, like presidents, find that their every utterance is recorded and analyzed. Scrutiny made some of them less likely to speak in public, while others used their platform to its fullest. They have campaigned for their husbands and other candidates. They have discussed political and social issues, promoted their own initiatives, detailed their goals, and touted their achievements. Some have been willing to talk about their families and life in the White House. They have answered questions, offered advice, and sent messages of comfort.

The words of the first ladies give us a glimpse into their private lives as well as their public personas. Some observances meant for family and friends reveal more of their unguarded personalities, while their public comments, delivered to inspire and influence, reveal their hopes and aspirations. Together they bring us greater understanding of the first ladies and their impact on their fellow Americans.

—*Lisa Kathleen Graddy, Curator, Political History*
Smithsonian's National Museum of American History

1. Diana B. Carlin, Anita B. McBride, and Nancy Kegan Smith, *Remember the First Ladies: The Legacies of America's History-Making Women* (Solana Beach, CA: Cognella Press, 2024, p. 376).

2. Clifton Truman Daniel, *Dear Harry, Love Bess: Bess Truman's Letters to Harry Truman 1919–1943* (Kirksville, MO, 2011).

3. Stacy A. Cordery, "Helen Herron Taft" in Lewis L. Gould, editor, *American First Ladies: Their Lives and Their Legacy* (New York: Routledge, 2021).

4. Edith P. Mayo and Denise D. Meringolo, *First Ladies: Political Role and Public Image* (Washington, DC: Smithsonian Institution, 1994).

EDITORIAL NOTE

Since the founding of the United States, every president has had an official hostess. Without one, propriety into the twentieth century forbade the president from including women at his parties and receptions. If the president was a bachelor or a widower, or if his wife was unable to fill or uninterested in the role of hostess, he chose another female family member or friend to serve instead.

This volume highlights the first ladies who acted as the official White House hostess during a presidential administration and also enjoyed the long-term social and political partnership that characterizes the role of first lady currently studied by the National Museum of American History. If quotations were not publicly available for a certain woman, we still included her information.

The quotations included in this volume have been corrected to be in modern English with American spellings for legibility. Furthermore, if a quotation comes from the memoir of a first lady, only the title and year of the book are given.

Gilbert Stuart painted Martha Washington from life in 1796 when the first couple resided in Philadelphia, then capital of the United States. This unattributed copy is based on Stuart's "Athaeneum" portrait.

❧ *Martha Washington* ❦

BORN: June 2, 1731
DIED: May 22, 1802
FIRST LADY: 1789–1797
wife of George Washington

I LIVE a very dull life here and know nothing that passes in the town. I never go to the public place . . . indeed I think I am more like a state prisoner than anything else. There are certain boundaries set for me which I must not depart from, and as I cannot do as I like I am obstinate and stay at home a great deal.
—*letter to her niece, Fanny Bassett Washington, on living in the president's residence in Philadelphia, October 23, 1789*

THOUGH the General's feelings and my own were perfectly in unison with respect to our predilection for private life, yet I cannot blame him for having acted according to his ideas of duty in obeying the voice of his country.
—*letter to a friend, Mercy Otis Warren, December 26, 1789*

I AM still determined to be cheerful and to be happy in whatever situation I may be; for I have also learnt from experience that the greater part of our happiness or misery depends on our dispositions, and not upon our circumstances.
—*letter to Mercy Otis Warren, December 26, 1789*

I PERSUADE myself to assure you, that with whatsoever pleasure your letters may be received, the satisfaction to be derived from them, will fall far short of that which your company would give.

—letter to a friend, Elizabeth Willing Powel,
December 17, 1797

I CANNOT be insensible to the mournful tributes of respect and veneration which are paid to the memory of my dear deceased Husband—and as his best services and most anxious wishes were always devoted to the welfare and happiness of his country—to know that they were truly appreciated and gratefully remembered affords no inconsiderable consolation.

—letter to John Adams about the death of her
husband, George Washington, December 27, 1799

❧ Abigail Adams ❧

BORN: November 11, 1744
DIED: October 28, 1818
FIRST LADY: 1797–1801
wife of John Adams

I WISH most sincerely there was not a slave in this province. It always appeared a most iniquitous scheme to me—to fight ourselves for what we are daily robbing and plundering from those who have as good a right to freedom as we have.

—letter to her husband, John Adams, September 24, 1774

I DESIRE you would Remember the Ladies, and be more generous and favorable to them than your ancestors. Do not put such unlimited power into the hands of the Husbands. Remember all Men would be tyrants if they could. If particular care and attention is not paid to the Ladies, we are determined to foment a Rebellion, and will not hold ourselves bound by any laws in which we have no voice, or representation.

—letter to John Adams, March 31, 1776

IF we mean to have heroes, statesmen and philosophers, we should have learned women.

—letter to John Adams, August 14, 1776

THE habits of a vigorous mind are formed in contending with difficulties. Great necessities call out great virtues.

—letter to her son, John Quincy Adams, January 19, 1780

LEARNING is not attained by chance, it must be sought for with ardor and attended to with diligence.

—letter to John Quincy Adams, May 8, 1780

I HAVE been so used to a freedom of sentiment that I know not how to place so many guards about me, as will be indispensable, to look at every word before I utter it, and to impose a silence upon my self, when I long to talk.

—letter to John Adams, about feeling constricted in her speech as the vice president's wife, February 20, 1796

I WILL never consent to have our sex considered in an inferior point of light. Let each planet shine in their own orbit. God and nature designed it so—If man is Lord, woman is *Lordess*.

I HAVE frequently said to my friends when they have thought me overburdened with cares; I had rather have too much, than too little. Life stagnates without action.

❧ *Dolley Madison* ❧

BORN: May 20, 1768
DIED: July 12, 1849
FIRST LADY: 1809–1817
wife of James Madison

A FEW hours only have passed since you left me my beloved, and I find nothing can relieve the oppression of my mind but speaking to you in this only way.

IT is one of my sources of happiness, never to desire a knowledge of other people's business.

HE enquired anxiously whether I had courage, or firmness to remain in the President's house until his return, on the morrow, or succeeding day, and on my assurance that I had no fear but for him and the success of our army, he left me, beseeching me to take care of myself, and of the cabinet papers, public and private.

—*letter to her sister, Lucy Todd, August 23, 1814*

Dolley Madison wrote to her sister about her preparations to leave Washington, DC, ahead of the British burning the city during the War of 1812.

OUR kind friend, Mr. Carroll, has come to hasten my departure, and is in a very bad humor with me because I insist on waiting until the large picture of Gen. Washington is secured, and it requires to be unscrewed from the wall. This process was found too tedious for these perilous moments; I have ordered the frame to be broken, and the canvas taken out—it is done; and the precious portrait placed in the hands of two gentlemen of New York, for safe keeping.

—*letter to Lucy Todd, August 23, 1814*

Following the defeat of American forces at the Battle of Bladensburg, the British army marched into Washington, DC, and set many buildings, including the White House and Capitol Building, ablaze. Dolley Madison was instructed to leave the White House, but refused to leave until a portrait of George Washington, known as the Lansdowne portrait, had been secured, thus saving the portrait.

THERE is one secret, however, she did not tell you, and that is the power we all have in forming our own destinies.
—*letter to her niece, Mary Estelle Elizabeth Cutts, August 1, 1833*

Dolley Madison's niece had sought the advice of a fortune-teller and was dismayed with her fortune.

❧ Elizabeth Monroe ❧

BORN: June 30, 1768
DIED: September 23, 1830
FIRST LADY: 1817–1825
wife of James Monroe

After her death, the letters and writings of Elizabeth Monroe were burned. Very few survive, and those that do are not publicly accessible.

❧ Louisa Adams ❧

BORN: February 12, 1775
DIED: May 15, 1852
FIRST LADY: 1825–1829
wife of John Quincy Adams

You know my friend I am not ambitious of anything but your affection and in that my wishes are unbounded.
—*letter to her husband, John Quincy Adams, July 4, 1796*

One of the duties of a first lady is to serve as hostess for the president.
This platter was used in state dinners hosted by Louisa Adams
during the presidency of her husband, John Quincy Adams.

OH! these visits they have made me sick many times and I really sometimes think they will make me crazy.
—*letter to her father-in-law, John Adams, January 4, 1820*

Louisa Adams was referring to paying and receiving calls or visits with the political wives and hostesses of Washington, DC.

THERE is something in this great unsocial house which depresses my spirits beyond expression and makes it impossible for me to feel at home or to fancy that I have a home any where.
—*letter to her son, George Washington Adams, about living in the White House, November 6, 1825*

I CANNOT believe there is any inferiority in the Sexes, as far as mind and intellect are concerned, and man is aware of the fact.
—*letter to her son, Charles Francis Adams, February 21, 1838*

I WAS carried through my journey and trials by the mercy of a kind Providence, and by the conviction that weakness, either of body or mind, would only render my difficulties greater and make matters worse.
—*"Mrs. John Quincy Adams's Narrative of a Journey from St. Petersburg to Paris in February, 1815"*

Louisa Adams's "Narrative" was published in *Scribner's Magazine*, October 1903.

❧ Letitia Tyler ❧

BORN: November 12, 1790
DIED: September 10, 1842
FIRST LADY: 1841–1842
first wife of John Tyler

No publicly available letters or writings of Letitia Tyler survive.

❧ Julia Tyler ❧

BORN: May 4, 1820
DIED: July 10, 1889
FIRST LADY: 1844–1845
second wife of John Tyler

WHEREVER we stopped, wherever we went, crowds of people outstripping one another, came to gaze at the President's wife. . . . The President says I am the best of diplomatists.

—*as quoted in* And Tyler Too: A Biography of John & Julia Gardiner Tyler *by Robert Seager, 1963*

I HAVE commenced my auspicious reign, and am in quiet possession of the Presidential Mansion.

—*as quoted in* And Tyler Too *by Robert Seager, 1963*

I VERY well know every eye is upon me, my dear mother, and I will behave accordingly.

—*letter to her mother, Juliana McLachlan-Gardiner, 1844, as quoted in* And Tyler Too *by Robert Seager, 1963*

❧ Sarah Polk ❧

BORN: September 4, 1803
DIED: August 14, 1891
FIRST LADY: 1845–1849
wife of James K. Polk

I DO not understand matters sufficiently well enough to form an opinion yet it does not strike me that it is the right thing for you to do.
—*letter to her husband, James K. Polk, December 31, 1840*

In 1840, James K. Polk was serving as the governor of Tennessee. Anticipating the death of Felix Grundy, the US Senator from Tennessee, politicians and prominent citizens privately wrote to Polk to express their views about who should fill the soon-to-be-vacant position. Sarah Polk passed these letters along, expressing that she did not agree with the choices suggested.

I AM not at all discouraged at anything I see in the papers or hear from any quarter, but when I think of the labor and fatigue you have to undergo I feel sad and melancholy, and conclude that success is not worth the labor.
—*letter to James K. Polk, about criticism he received as governor of Tennessee, April 8, 1841*

I CANNOT find fault now with the ladies for going away from home so much, because I went so often with Mr. Polk. . . . He always wished me to go, and he would say, "Why should you stay at home? To take care of the house? Why, if the house burns down, we can live without it."

—*as quoted in* Memorials of Sarah Childress Polk: Wife of the Eleventh President of the United States, *by Anson and Fanny Nelson, 1892*

IF I should be so fortunate as to reach the White House, I expect to live on twenty-five thousand dollars a year, and I will neither keep house nor make butter.

—*as quoted in* Memorials of Sarah Childress Polk *by Anson and Fanny Nelson, 1892*

I DID not desire this distinction to be made between others and myself. . . . I did not wish for the attention. I always had so much that I could not wish for more.

—*on being treated differently as first lady, as quoted in* Memorials of Sarah Childress Polk *by Anson and Fanny Nelson, 1892*

I AM astonished at so much attention being paid me, an old woman on the verge of the grave. I recognize nothing in myself; I am only an atom in the hands of God, who does it all.

—*as quoted in* Memorials of Sarah Childress Polk *by Anson and Fanny Nelson, 1892*

❧ Abigail Fillmore ❧

BORN: March 13, 1798
DIED: March 30, 1853
FIRST LADY: 1850–1853
wife of Millard Fillmore

No publicly available letters or writings of Abigail Fillmore survive.

❧ Jane Pierce ❧

BORN: March 12, 1806
DIED: December 2, 1863
FIRST LADY: 1853–1857
wife of Franklin Pierce

OH how I wish he was out of political life. How much better it would be for him on every count.
—*as quoted in* Franklin Pierce: Young Hickory of the Granite Hills *by Roy Franklin Nichols, 1931*

I cannot believe who I was when I was in the White House. I am a completely different person.
—*as quoted in* Franklin Pierce *by Roy Franklin Nichols, 1931*

❧ *Harriet Lane* ❧

BORN: May 9, 1830
DIED July 3, 1903
FIRST LADY: 1857–1861
niece of James Buchanan

I WAS a young girl, so uncle often waived the social conventionalities which hedged in the presiding lady of the mansion. He permitted me to go to private balls, which were then the rage in fashionable society. But all the prerogatives of the lady of the White House were accorded without dissent by the great ladies of the social world during those brilliant days at Washington.

—*as quoted in "Harriet Lane, First Lady: Hostess Extraordinary in Difficult Times," by Homer T. Rosenberger,* Records of the Columbia Historical Society, *Vol. 66/68, 1966/1968*

❧ *Mary Lincoln* ❧

BORN: December 13, 1818
DIED: July 16, 1882
FIRST LADY: 1861–1865
wife of Abraham Lincoln

THAT most difficult of all problems to solve, my evil genius Procrastination has whispered to me to tarry til a more convenient season.

—*letter to a friend, Mercy Anne Levering, June 1841*

THE President at every reception selects a lady to lead the promenade with him. Now it occurs to me that this custom is an absurd one. On such occasions our guests recognize the position of President as first of all; consequently he takes the lead in everything; well now, if they recognize his position, they should also recognize mine. I am his wife.

—*as quoted in* Behind the Scenes
by Elizabeth Keckly, 1868

Elizabeth Keckly was the dressmaker for and confidante of Mary Todd Lincoln.

TELL me, how can I live, without my Husband, any longer? This is my first awakening thought, each morning, & as I watch the waves of the turbulent lake, under our windows, I sometimes feel I should like to go under them.

—*letter to a friend, Elizabeth Blair Lee,*
after the assassination of her husband, July 11, 1865

I AM convinced, the longer I live, that life & its blessings are not so entirely unjustly distributed, [as] when we are suffering greatly, we are inclined to suppose.

—*letter to a friend, Eliza Slataper, December 13, 1868*

TROUBLE comes soon enough, my dear child, and you must enjoy life, whenever you can.

—*letter to her daughter-in-law, Mary Harlan Lincoln,*
March 22, 1869

Mary Todd Lincoln never stopped mourning her husband
Abraham Lincoln after his assassination in 1865.
She wore mourning clothes and used this black onyx lapel watch
as her personal timepiece for the remainder of her life.

❧ Julia Grant ❧

BORN: January 26, 1826
DIED: December 14, 1902
FIRST LADY: 1869–1877
wife of Ulysses S. Grant

I ALWAYS knew my husband would rise in the world. I believed he would someday inhabit the highest office in the land. I felt this even when we were newly married, and he was making a mere pittance in salary.
—*"Widow of General Grant 'Grants' an Interview,"*
Missouri Republican, *April 27, 1900*

❧ Lucy Hayes ❧

BORN: August 28, 1831
DIED: June 25, 1889
FIRST LADY: 1877–1881
wife of Rutherford B. Hayes

THE Northern heart is truly fired—the enthusiasm that prevails in our city is perfectly irresistible. . . . Those who favor secession or even sympathy with the South find it prudent to be quiet.
—*letter to her husband, Rutherford B. Hayes, April 15, 1861*

In this letter, Lucy Webb Hayes discussed the sentiments of citizens in Cincinnati, Ohio, about the Civil War, which had begun just three days prior.

I FELT as most in the house did—that Justice and Mercy should go together.

—*letter to Rutherford B. Hayes, April 17, 1865*

Lucy Webb Hayes noted her negative feelings about the secessionists toward the end of the Civil War, stating that she agreed with those in the meeting house listening to a speech calling for justice for secessionists, not just mercy.

WITHOUT intending to be public, I find myself, for a quiet, mind-her-own-business woman, rather notorious.

—*letter to one of her sons, as quoted in* First Lady: The Life of Lucy Webb Hayes *by Emily Apt Greer, 1984*

❧ Lucretia Garfield ❧

BORN: April 19, 1832
DIED: March 14, 1918
FIRST LADY: 1881
wife of James Garfield

AFTER a short pause the President-elect stood out before the people and with the inspiration of the time and the occasion lifting him up into his fullest grandeur he became in the magnificence with which he pronounced his Inaugural almost superhuman.

—*diary entry about the inauguration of her husband, James Garfield, March 4, 1881*

USE SULPHUR BITTERS.

Mrs. President Cleveland.

The nation was captivated with the young, beautiful first lady Frances Cleveland after her marriage to sitting president Grover Cleveland in 1886. Her popularity inspired advertisers to exploit her image, using her likeness to sell their products.

ONLY two months ago this day he was living—looking up into my eyes, talking to me so tenderly of my care of him—so near to me in every way, and yet, since that same night when his spirit went out, an age of loneliness and bitter anguish seems to have intervened.
—*letter to a friend, Alice, November 19, 1881*

❧ *Frances Cleveland* ❦

BORN: July 21, 1864
DIED: October 29, 1947
FIRST LADY: 1886–1889 and 1893–1897
wife of Grover Cleveland

I CAN wish the women of our country no greater blessing than that their homes and their lives may be as happy and that their husbands may be as kind, attentive, considerate and affectionate as mine.
—*from a letter to a correspondent, as published in the* Fort Scott Daily Tribune, *June 7, 1888*

Frances Cleveland issued this statement to the press after Democratic opponents of Grover Cleveland circulated rumors that he hit her.

I HAVE not had a life yet. It is all before me.
—*as quoted in* The New York Times, *March 4, 1889*

I WANT you to take good care of all the furniture and ornaments in the house, and not let any of them get lost or broken, for I want to find everything just as it is now, when we come back again. . . . We are coming back just four years from today.

—*as quoted in* Memories of the White House: The Home Life of Our Presidents from Lincoln to Roosevelt *by William H. Crook, 1911*

Frances Cleveland made this remark upon leaving the White House at the end of her husband's first term. Four years later, Grover Cleveland was re-elected as president, and the Clevelands returned to the White House.

I FIND myself very busy with my "social duties" beginning again and two babies. I give so much time to the children because I won't be cheated of their babyhood by anything—much less "not worth-while things."

—*letter to a friend, Helena Gilder, December 15, 1893*

❧ Caroline Harrison ☙

BORN: October 1, 1832
DIED: October 25, 1892
FIRST LADY: 1889–1892
wife of Benjamin Harrison

VERY few people understand to what straits the President's family has been put at times for lack of accommodations. Really, there are only five sleeping apartments and there is no feeling of privacy.

—*as quoted in* The Story of the White House *by Esther Singleton, 1907*

SINCE this society has been organized and so much thought and reading directed to the early struggles of this country, it has been made plain that much of its success was due to the character of the women of that era. The unselfish part they acted constantly commends itself to our admiration and example.
—*speech at the first Daughters of the American Revolution Continental Congress, February 22, 1892*

✣ *Ida McKinley* ✣

BORN: June 8, 1847
DIED: May 26, 1907
FIRST LADY: 1897–1901
wife of William McKinley

YOUNG people are always on the go, always out, always coming in late.
—*as quoted in* President McKinley: Architect of the American Century *by Robert W. Merry, 2017*

I REALIZE more and more that I am not company for anyone but I do not wish to forget my friends. I am more lonely every day I live.
—*letter to a friend, Webb C. Hayes, December 10, 1905*

❧ Edith Roosevelt ☙

BORN: August 6, 1861
DIED: September 30, 1948
FIRST LADY: 1901–1909
wife of Theodore Roosevelt

I THINK imagination is one of the greatest blessings of life, and while one can lose oneself in a book one can never be thoroughly unhappy.
—*letter to her husband, Theodore Roosevelt, June 8, 1886*

I LOVE you with all the passion of a girl who has never loved before, and please be patient with me when I cannot put my heart on paper.
—*letter to Theodore Roosevelt, June 8, 1886*

❧ Helen "Nellie" Taft ☙

BORN: June 2, 1861
DIED: May 22, 1943
FIRST LADY: 1909–1913
wife of William Howard Taft

I CONFESS only to a lively interest in my husband's work which I experienced from the beginning of our association and which nothing in our long life together, neither monotony, nor illness, nor misfortune, has served to lessen.
—*from* Recollections of Full Years, *1914*

SINCE the ex-President was not going to ride back to the White House with his successor, I decided that I would. No President's wife had ever done it before, but as long as precedents were being disregarded I thought it might not be too great a risk for me to disregard this one. . . . I had my way and in spite of protests took my place at my husband's side.

—*from* Recollections of Full Years, *1914*

Nellie Taft reminisced about the memorable ride with her husband, William Howard Taft, on the day of his inauguration after Theodore Roosevelt refused to follow the tradition of riding to the White House with his successor.

MY very active participation in my husband's career came to an end when he became President. I always had the satisfaction of knowing almost as much as he about the politics and the intricacies of any situation in which he found himself, and my life was filled with interests of a most unusual kind. But in the White House I found my own duties too engrossing to permit me to follow him long or very far into the governmental maze which soon enveloped him.

—*from* Recollections of Full Years, *1914*

THE woman's voice is the voice of wisdom and I can see nothing unwomanly in her casting the ballot.

—*as quoted in* The Bully Pulpit: Theodore Roosevelt, William Howard Taft, and the Golden Age of Journalism *by Doris Kearns Goodwin, 2013*

❧ Ellen Wilson ❧

BORN: May 15, 1860
DIED: August 6, 1914
FIRST LADY: 1913–1914
first wife of Woodrow Wilson

I AM not afraid of criticism.
>—*letter to her husband, Woodrow Wilson, 1884*

I COULD not love anyone whom I did not admire and look up to and believe in wholly.
>—*letter to Woodrow Wilson, May 12, 1885*

I AM naturally the most unambitious of women and life in the White House has no attractions for me. Quite the contrary in fact!
>—*letter to former president William Howard Taft*
>*January 10, 1913*

In response to to a letter Taft had written her offering advice about life in the White House, Ellen Wilson wrote him about her husband's election and their upcoming move to Washington, DC.

MY life has been the most remarkable life history that I ever even read about—and to think I have lived it with you!
>—*letter to Woodrow Wilson, October 5, 1913*

❧ Edith Wilson ❧

BORN: October 15, 1872
DIED: December 28, 1961
FIRST LADY: 1915–1921
second wife of Woodrow Wilson

I FEEL that I am sharing your work and being taken into a partnership, as it were.
— *letter to her husband, Woodrow Wilson, June 18, 1915*

I, MYSELF, never made a single decision regarding the disposition of public affairs. The only decision that was mine was what was important and what was not, and the very important decision of when to present matters to my husband.

—*from* My Memoir, *1939*

In her memoir, Edith Wilson disputed prevalent rumors that she acted as president while her husband was incapacitated by making decisions and signing his name to documents.

Two hours later, at three A.M., Monday, November 11th, came the long-awaited news—the Armistice was signed! The guns were still! The World War was ended!

—*from* My Memoir, *1939*

THE only fear Woodrow Wilson knew was the fear of God should he fail in his own duty.

—*from* My Memoir, *1939*

❧ Florence Harding ❧

BORN: August 15, 1860
DIED: November 21, 1924
FIRST LADY: 1921–1923
wife of Warren G. Harding

I AM content to bask in my husband's limelight, but I cannot see why anyone should want to be President in the next four years.

> —*comments to reporters at the Republican nominating convention, June 10, 1920*

OH, I know you think I'm boasting, but I have had only one fad, the only fad I have had for the last twenty-six years, and that is my husband.

> —*comments to reporters, June 12, 1920*

THERE is utmost need for effective and unremitting effort at organization, education, and civic training among women. They have come suddenly into a mighty responsibility for the national interest.

> —*letter to US Representative Arthur Livermore about women gaining the right to vote in 1919, January 13, 1922*

I ALWAYS take a particular interest in the activities of newspaper women, because I have regarded myself as quite one of them for a great many years.

> —*letter to the New York Women's Newspaper Club, April 9, 1922*

❦ Grace Coolidge ❦

BORN: January 3, 1879
DIED: July 8, 1957
FIRST LADY: 1923–1929
wife of Calvin Coolidge

DAILY I am impressed anew with the responsibility and opportunity which has been given me. In no sense does it overwhelm me, rather does it inspire me and increase my energy and I am so filled with the desire to measure up.

—*diary entry during her tenure as first lady*

THERE was a sense of detachment. This was I, and yet not I—this was the wife of the President and she took precedence over me; my personal likes and dislikes must be subordinated to the consideration of those things which were required of her. In like manner this man at whose side I walked was the President of our great country; his first duty was to its people. It therefore became quite natural to refer to him as "the president" and to address him as "Mr. President" in the presence of others.

—*from* Grace Coolidge: An Autobiography, *1992*

I FOUND that the domestic problems of the mistress of the White House were not different from those of the housewife of any well-run household.

—*from* Grace Coolidge, *1992*

❧ Lou Hoover ❧

BORN: March 29, 1874
DIED: January 7, 1944
FIRST LADY: 1929–1933
wife of Herbert Hoover

THE happiest part of my own very happy childhood and girlhood was without doubt the hours and days, the sometimes entire months, which I spent in pseudo-pioneering, or scouting in our wonderful western mountains with my father in our vacation times. So I cannot but want every girl to have the same widening, simplifying joy-getting influences in her own life.

> —*speech to the Girl Scouts of America upon becoming the group's president, January 24, 1922*

WOMEN have come to stay in politics. There is no way of keeping out and there is no such thing as a neutral or passive voice. If you are not active, you are helping the other side.

> —*remarks at the annual meeting of Pennsylvania Republican Women, as quoted in the* Philadelphia Record, *May 5, 1923*

DON'T let amusement hours "just happen." For your future is almost as dependent on what you do in your periods of re-creating, a recreation, as in those of your creating efforts.

> —*radio speech to 4-H clubs, November 7, 1931*

❧ Eleanor Roosevelt ❧

BORN: October 11, 1884
DIED: November 7, 1962
FIRST LADY: 1933–1945
wife of Franklin D. Roosevelt

A SNUB is the effort of a person who feels superior to make someone else feel inferior. To do so, he has to find someone who can be made to feel inferior.
—*response to reporters at a press conference, 1935*

THE most important thing in any relationship is not what you get but what you give.
—*from* This Is My Story, *1937*

WHATEVER is asked of us, I am sure we can accomplish it. We are the free and unconquerable people of the United States of America.
—*address to the nation after the bombing of Pearl Harbor, December 7, 1941*

ONE of the blessings of age is to learn not to part on a note of sharpness, to treasure the moments spent with those we love, and to make them whenever possible good to remember, for time is short.
—*My Day, February 5, 1943*

My Day was a national syndicated newspaper column written by Eleanor Roosevelt from 1935 until 1962.

At all times, day by day, we have to continue fighting for freedom of religion, freedom of speech, and freedom from want—for these are things that must be gained in peace as well as in war.

—*My Day, April 15, 1943*

When will our consciences grow so tender that we will act to prevent human misery rather than avenge it?

—*My Day, February 16, 1946*

It isn't enough to talk about peace. One must believe in it. And it isn't enough to believe in it. One must work at it.

—*Voice of America broadcast, November 11, 1951*

Where, after all, do universal human rights begin? In small places, close to home—so close and so small that they cannot be seen on any maps of the world. Yet they are the world of the individual person; the neighborhood he lives in; the school or college he attends; the factory, farm or office where he works. Such are the places where every man, woman and child seeks equal justice, equal opportunity, equal dignity without discrimination. Unless these rights have meaning there, they have little meaning anywhere. Without concerned citizen action to uphold them close to home, we shall look in vain for progress in the larger world.

—*"The Great Question," remarks delivered at the United Nations in New York, March 27, 1958*

SURELY, in the light of history, it is more intelligent to hope rather than to fear, to try rather than not to try. For one thing we know beyond all doubt: Nothing has ever been achieved by the person who says, "It can't be done."

—*from* You Learn by Living, *1960*

❧ Elizabeth "Bess" Truman ❧

BORN: February 13, 1885
DIED: October 18, 1982
FIRST LADY: 1945–1953
wife of Harry S. Truman

A WOMAN's place in public is to sit beside her husband, be silent, and be sure her hat is on straight.

—*as quoted in* Bess W. Truman
by Margaret Truman Daniel, 1986

I'M only the president's wife and the mother of his daughter.

—*as quoted in* Harry S. Truman and the
News Media: Contentious Relations, Belated
Respect *by Franklin D. Mitchell, 1998*

✎ Mamie Eisenhower ✎

BORN: November 14, 1896
DIED: November 1, 1979
FIRST LADY: 1953–1961
wife of Dwight D. Eisenhower

OF course, being mistress of the White House is a terrific responsibility, and I am truly grateful for my Army wife training.
　　—*letter to a friend, Nanette Kutner, November 15, 1952*

WE women have to have a voice in things.
　　—*as quoted in* The Pittsburgh Press, *April 22, 1955*

Mamie Eisenhower said this in support of a friend, Ellen Harris, who was running for a seat in the House of Representatives.

I HAD but one career, and its name is Ike.
　　　　　　—*as quoted in* Upstairs at the White House:
　　　　　　My Life with the First Ladies *by*
　　　　　　J. B. West and Mary Lynn Kotz, 1973

I'VE just had the first good night's sleep I've had since we've been in the White House. Our new bed finally got here, and now I can reach over and pat Ike on his old bald head any time I want to!
　　　　　　—*as quoted in* Upstairs at the White House
　　　　　　by J. B. West and Mary Lynn Kotz, 1973

❧ Jacqueline Kennedy ❧

BORN: July 28, 1929
DIED: May 19, 1994
FIRST LADY: 1961–1963
wife of John F. Kennedy

EVERYWHERE, peace is uppermost in women's minds. They say if we can't keep the peace, then other issues aren't important.
> —*on peace and her husband's campaign, interview with Henry Fonda, CBS, November 2, 1960*

IT would be sacrilege merely to "redecorate" it—a word I hate. It must be restored—that has nothing to do with decoration. That is a question of scholarship.
> —*about the White House, in an interview with Hugh Sidey, September 1, 1961*

No fathers or mothers can be happy until they have the possibility of jobs and education for their children. This must be for all and not just a fortunate few.
> —*speech at La Morita, Venezuela, December 16, 1961*

I FELT as though I had just turned into a piece of public property. It's frightening to lose your anonymity at thirty-one.
> —*as quoted in the* Des Moines Register, *July 22, 1962*

Jacqueline Kennedy commented on her position as first lady after her husband's inauguration.

I THINK that I should have known that he was magic all along. I did know it—but I should have guessed that it would be too much to ask to grow old with him and see our children grow up together. So now, he is a legend when he would have preferred to be a man.

—from an essay for Look *magazine, November 17, 1964*

Jacqueline Kennedy wrote an article for the JFK Memorial Issue of *Look* magazine, commemorating the life of her husband a year after his assassination.

ONE man can make a difference and every man should try.

*—written for a traveling exhibition when
the John F. Kennedy Library opened, 1979*

✖ *Claudia "Lady Bird" Johnson* ✖

BORN: December 22, 1912
DIED: July 11, 2007
FIRST LADY: 1963–1969
wife of Lyndon B. Johnson

THE last few months have taught us that Civil Rights is not a problem peculiar to the South, but a problem all over the country.

*—transcript of tape about her thoughts
on her whistle-stop tour, October 1964*

In 1964, Lady Bird Johnson took a train, called the Lady Bird Special, and went on a tour of eight southern states to talk about the Civil Rights Act, making forty-seven stops in just four days.

WHERE flowers bloom, so does hope—and hope is the precious, indispensable ingredient without which the war on poverty can never be won.

—*remarks at the annual convention of the Associated Press Managing Editors Association, October 1, 1965*

FOR the environment after all is where we all meet, where we all have a mutual interest. It is one thing that all of us share. It is not only a mirror of ourselves, but a focusing lens on what we can become.

—*diary entry, October 9, 1967*

I KNOW that the nature we are concerned with ultimately is human nature. That is the point of the beautification movement, and that finally is the point of architecture. Winston Churchill said, "First we shape our buildings, and then they shape us." The same is true of our highways, our parks, our public buildings, the environment we create. They shape us.

—*B. Y. Morrison Lecture at the American Institute of Architects annual convention in Portland, Oregon, June 26, 1968*

IT'S odd that you can get so anesthetized by your own pain or your own problem that you don't quite fully share the hell of someone close to you.

—*from* A White House Diary, *1970*

MY heart found its home long ago in the beauty, mystery, order, and disorder of the flowering earth.

—*letter in* Native Plants *magazine, Fall 2002*

❧ Patricia "Pat" Nixon ❧

BORN: March 16, 1912
DIED: June 22, 1993
FIRST LADY: 1969–1974
wife of Richard M. Nixon

I AM more convinced than ever that if you run it will be a terrible mistake. But if you weigh everything and still decide to run, I will support your decision.
—*from* RN: The Memoirs of Richard Nixon
by Richard Nixon, 1978

I THINK a person has to just be herself.
—*"In Your Heart You Know He's Nixon,"*
article in New York *magazine, October 28, 1968*

I HAVEN'T just sat back and thought of myself or my ideas or what I wanted to do. Oh no, I've stayed interested in people. I've kept working.
—*"In Your Heart You Know He's Nixon,"*
New York *magazine, October 28, 1968*

BEING First Lady is the hardest unpaid job in the world.
—*news conference, January 1972*

IF I had a choice, I'd rather be admired less and have my husband tormented less. I'd prefer that people concentrate on a fair assessment of him and his Presidency.
—*reaction to being voted most-admired woman*
in a recent poll, Newsweek, *Volume 85, 1975*

Candidates' wives and first ladies sometimes use their
popularity to help their husbands' campaigns. Pat Nixon was
the first candidate's wife to "run" for first lady,
even hosting an event to promote "Pat for First Lady."

❧ Elizabeth "Betty" Ford ❧

BORN: April 8, 1918
DIED: July 8, 2011
FIRST LADY: 1974–1977
wife of Gerald R. Ford

WHEN other women have this same operation, it doesn't make any headlines. But the fact that I was the wife of the President put it in headlines and brought before the public this particular experience I was going through. It made a lot of women realize that it could happen to them. I'm sure I've saved at least one person—maybe more.

> —*as quoted in "Breast Cancer: Fear and Facts,"*
> *in* Time *magazine, November 4, 1974*

Betty Ford provided this explanation for her reasoning behind the decision to announce her breast cancer diagnosis to the nation.

I FEEL that the liberated woman is the woman who is happy doing what she's doing, whether it's a job or as a housewife, it doesn't make a bit of difference. Just so she, inwardly, feels that she is happy and that she is liberated.

> —*"On the Hardest Part of Being the First Lady,"*
> *interview with 60 Minutes, August 1975*

I DO not believe that being first lady should prevent me from expressing my views. . . . Being ladylike does not require silence.

> —*remarks to the International Women's Year*
> *Conference in Cleveland, Ohio, October 25, 1975*

I WAS very unprepared to be a political wife, but I d
worry because I really didn't think he was goin
win. At that time, only old men went to Congress
—*from* The Times of My Life, *1*

I FIGURED, okay, I'll move to the White House,
the best I can, and if they don't like it, they can ki
me out, but they can't make me somebody I'm not.
—*from* The Times of My Life, *19*

❧ *Rosalynn Carter* ❧

BORN: August 18, 1927
DIED: November 19, 2023
FIRST LADY: 1977–1981
wife of James "Jimmy" Carter

A FIRST lady is in a position to know the needs of the
country and do something about them. She can have
real influence. It would be a shame not to take advan-
tage of the power. I think that the wives of Presidents
need to be informed and to speak out on matters that
are important to them. I intend to do that.
— *"One Perfect Rosalynn," article in the*
New York Daily News, *October 25, 1976*

JIMMY and I were always partners.
— *"Mrs. Carter Speaks Out," article*
in The New York Times, *June 14, 1983*

I HAD already learned from more than a decade of political life that I was going to be criticized no matter what I did, so I might as well be criticized for something I wanted to do.

—*from* First Lady from Plains, *1984*

MY greatest disappointment in all the projects I worked on during the White House years was the failure of the Equal Rights Amendment to be ratified.

—*from* First Lady from Plains, *1984*

The Equal Rights Amendment would have amended the United States Constitution to guarantee equal legal rights for all American citizens regardless of sex. Congress set a ratification deadline of March 22, 1979, that failed to be met, with only thirty-five of the necessary thirty-eight states ratifying the amendment.

THE political victories for women were important ones, and being a woman who mattered pleased me very much during my time as First Lady. But I never forgot that I was there because my husband held his high office, not because I had been elected. I had helped him get there, and I liked to think he couldn't have done it without me, but the situation was clearly the same one women have faced for centuries. First Ladies throughout our history have been expected to be adoring wives and perfect mothers, to manage the public and social aspects of the White House to the satisfaction of all critics, and to participate in "appropriate public service." The role of First Lady is a difficult—

and sometimes nearly impossible—one to fill, and each one of us has dealt with this challenge in her own way.
—*from* First Lady from Plains, *1984*

❧ *Nancy Reagan* ❧

BORN: July 6, 1921
DIED: March 6, 2016
FIRST LADY: 1981–1989
wife of Ronald Reagan

DRUGS steal away so much. They take and take, until finally every time a drug goes into a child, something else is forced out—like love and hope and trust and confidence. Drugs take away the dream from every child's heart and replace it with a nightmare, and it's time we in America stand up and replace those dreams.
— *"Just Say No" address, September 14, 1986*

"Just Say No" was a popular slogan created by Nancy Reagan as part of the US-led "war on drugs," a global campaign to encourage drug prohibition and reduce the illegal drug trade.

WHILE I loved being first lady, my eight years with that title were the most difficult years of my life.
— *from* My Turn: The Memoirs of Nancy Reagan, *1989*

I'M the one who knows him best, and I was the only person in the White House who had absolutely no agenda of her own—except helping him. And so I make no apologies for telling him what I thought.

Just because you're married doesn't mean you have no right to express your opinions. For eight years I was sleeping with the president, and if that doesn't give you special access, I don't know what does!
—*from* My Turn, *1989*

Our relationship is very special. We were very much in love and still are. Thank God we found each other. When I say my life began with Ronnie, well, it's true. It did. Forty-six years? Can't imagine life without him.
—*"Ronnie & Nancy," interview with* Vanity Fair,
July 1998

❧ *Barbara Bush* ❧

BORN: June 8, 1925
DIED: April 17, 2018
FIRST LADY: 1989–1993
wife of George H. W. Bush

I DON'T agree with George Bush on every issue, and I don't expect him to agree with me on every issue . . . but we are in agreement on most of the important things.
—*interview with* The New York Times,
February 22, 1981

EVERYTHING I worry about would be better if more people could read, write, and comprehend.
—*"Barbara Bush Tends His Image Her Way,"*
interview in The New York Times, *May 5, 1988*

AT the end of your life, you will never regret not having passed one more test, not winning one more verdict or not closing one more deal. You will regret time not spent with a husband, a friend, a child, or a parent.

—commencement address at Wellesley College,
June 1, 1990

FOR heaven's sake enjoy life. Don't cry over things that were or things that aren't. Enjoy what you have now to the fullest. In all honesty you really only have two choices; you can like what you do *or* you can dislike it.

—from Barbara Bush: A Memoir, *1994*

GEORGE BUSH and I have been the two luckiest people in the world, and when all the dust has settled and all the crowds are gone, the things that matter are faith, family and friends. We have been inordinately blessed, and we know that.

—from Barbara Bush, *1994*

THE First Lady is going to be criticized no matter what she does. If she does too little. If she does too much. And I think you just have to be yourself and do the best you can.

—interview at An Evening with
Former First Ladies, C-SPAN, March 9, 1998

❧ Hillary Clinton ❧

BORN: October 26, 1947
FIRST LADY: 1993–2001
wife of William J. "Bill" Clinton

I SUPPOSE I could have stayed home and baked cookies
and had teas, but what I decided to do was to fulfill
my profession which I entered before my husband was
in public life.
> —*response to a reporter's questions about her career,*
> *March 16, 1992*

You know, everybody has setbacks in their life, and
everybody falls short of whatever goals they might set
for themselves. That's part of living and coming to
terms with who you are as a person.
> —*interview with* People *magazine, December 28, 1992*

IF there is one message that echoes forth from this conference, let it be that human rights are women's rights
and women's rights are human rights once and for all.
> —*remarks to the United Nations' fourth World Conference*
> *on Women in Beijing, China, September 5, 1995*

WE should remember that just as a positive outlook
on life can promote good health, so can everyday acts
of kindness.
> —*from* It Takes a Village: And Other
> Lessons Children Teach Us, *1996*

LIKE it or not, women are always subject to criticism if they show too much feeling in public.

—from Living History, *2003*

THE American character is both idealistic and realistic: why can't our government reflect both?

—remarks to the Senate's Council on Foreign Relations, October 31, 2006

ALTHOUGH we weren't able to shatter that highest, hardest glass ceiling this time, thanks to you, it's got about 18 million cracks in it.

—concession speech after losing the Democratic presidential primary to Barack Obama, June 7, 2008

TONIGHT, we've reached a milestone in our nation's march toward a more perfect union: the first time that a major party has nominated a woman for President. Standing here as my mother's daughter, and my daughter's mother, I'm so happy this day has come. Happy for grandmothers and little girls and everyone in between. Happy for boys and men, too—because when any barrier falls in America, for anyone, it clears the way for everyone.

—speech upon accepting the Democratic party presidential nomination at the Democratic National Convention, July 28, 2016

❧ Laura Bush ❧

BORN: November 4, 1946
FIRST LADY: 2001–2009
wife of George W. Bush

I LOVE to read, and I want more Americans to experience the sense of adventure and satisfaction that comes from reading a good book.
—*speech at the first annual National Book Festival,*
September 7, 2001

IT'S incumbent upon us as adults and teachers and principals and community leaders to make sure we're doing the very best we can for our children.
—*press conference, May 19, 2004*

Laura Bush engaged reporters following a visit to William Walker Elementary School in Beaverton, Oregon.

I'M not wild about the term first lady. I'd just like to be called Laura Bush.
—*"Laura Bush Grows into Star Role,"*
interview with CBS News, June 24, 2004

WE talk about issues, but I'm not his adviser, I'm his wife . . . I find that it's really best not to give your spouse a lot of advice. I don't want a lot of advice from him.
—*"Laura Bush Grows into Star Role,"*
CBS News, June 24, 2004

In the United States, the presidency is not just about one person. The presidency is about all of the people who join with that president in years of service to our remarkable nation. They are the people who never fly on Air Force One, but who put in countless late nights and earlier mornings, who spend less time with their family and friends and more time hard at work caring for our country. The presidency is about the men and women of our military who serve every president and who make the ultimate sacrifice to protect us and keep us safe. The stones in the walls represent your years of service. This building is here because of your service and for that, George and I thank you from the bottom of our hearts.

—remarks at the dedication of the George W. Bush
Presidential Center in Dallas, Texas, April 25, 2013

❧ *Michelle Obama* ☙

BORN: January 17, 1964
FIRST LADY: 2009–2017
wife of Barack Obama

EVERY day, the people I meet inspire me, every day, they make me proud, every day they remind me how blessed we are to live in the greatest nation on earth.

—speech at the Democratic National Convention,
September 4, 2012

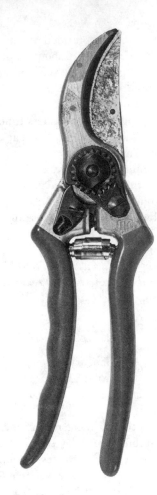

Michelle Obama often focused on healthier eating, exercise, and childhood obesity during her tenure as first lady. She planted the White House Kitchen Garden in 2009 and used these shears when tending to the garden.

WHEN you've worked hard, and done well, and walked through that doorway of opportunity . . . you do not slam it shut behind you . . . you reach back, and you give other folks the same chances that helped you succeed.

—*speech at the Democratic National Convention,*
September 4, 2012

I WAKE up every morning in a house that was built by slaves. And I watch my daughters, two beautiful, intelligent, black young women playing with their dogs on the White House lawn.

—*speech at the Democratic National Convention,*
July 25, 2016

You cannot take your freedoms for granted. Just like generations who have come before you, you have to do your part to preserve and protect those freedoms.

—*remarks at the National School Counselor*
of the Year event, January 6, 2017

Now I think it's one of the most useless questions an adult can ask a child—What do you want to be when you grow up? As if growing up is finite. As if at some point you become something and that's the end.

—*from* Becoming, *2018*

WHAT truly makes our country great is its diversity. I've seen that beauty in so many ways over the years. Whether we are born here or seek refuge here, there's a place for us all. We must remember it's not my America or your America. It's our America.

—post from Michelle Obama (@MichelleObama)
on the social media platform Twitter, July 19, 2019

❧ *Melania Trump* ❧

BORN: April 26, 1970
FIRST LADY: 2017–2021
wife of Donald J. Trump

YOU judge a society by how it treats its citizens. We must do our best to ensure that every child can live in comfort and security, with the best possible education.

—speech at the Republican National Convention,
July 18, 2016

ON July 28th, 2006, I was very proud to become a citizen of the United States—the greatest privilege on planet Earth. I cannot, or will not, take the freedoms this country offers for granted.

—speech at the Republican National Convention,
July 18, 2016

WE are responsible for empowering our next generation with values.

— post from Melania Trump (@FLOTUS45)
on the social media platform Twitter, February 11, 2017

BE passionate in everything you do but always remember that violence is never the answer and will never be justified.

—farewell message, January 18, 2021

❧ Jill Biden ❧

BORN: June 3, 1951
FIRST LADY: 2021–
wife of Joseph R. "Joe" Biden

I'M not a politician. I am an English teacher.
—"Just Asking: Jill Biden Talks about 2016, Teaching and Running with the Secret Service," interview in The Washington Post, *April 11, 2014*

EDUCATION teaches us compassion and kindness, connection to others. Education doesn't just make us smarter. It makes us whole.
—Cubberley Lecture at Stanford University, May 9, 2018

THIS is the truest thing I know: that love makes a family whole. It doesn't matter if you're blending a family with biological and nonbiological children, or healing the wounds of losing a loved one, or inviting an aging parent to live with you. The details may differ, but love is the common denominator.
—from Where the Light Enters: Building a Family, Discovering Myself, *2019*

It shouldn't take courage to be yourself. It shouldn't take courage to go to school and walk down the halls as the person you know you are. It shouldn't take courage to hold the hand of the person you love on a bus, to kiss them goodbye on the sidewalk, to share one of the most fundamental and beautiful connections that any one of us can have in this life. It shouldn't but, too often and in too many places, it still does. And in some way, all of you here today have called on that courage. And you've used your voice to say: We will not go back. We will not let the progress that we've fought for slip away.

—remarks at a reception to celebrate Pride month,
June 15, 2022

Though the tradition had been to have portraits of Presidents in the East Wing—which houses the Office of the First Lady—I lined the halls with portraits of the women who came before me. They all made their mark on our country, defining the undefined role of the First Lady in their own way.

—remarks at a White House Historical Association gala,
November 3, 2023